Clovis Crawfish and the Curious Crapaud

THE CLOVIS CRAWFISH SERIES

Clovis Crawfish and the Big Betail
(1963)

Clovis Crawfish and the Spinning Spider
(1966)

Clovis Crawfish and Michelle Mantis
(1975)

Clovis Crawfish and the Singing Cigales
(1981)

Clovis Crawfish and the Orphan Zo-Zo
(1983)

Clovis Crawfish and Petit Papillon
(1984)

Clovis Crawfish and Etienne Escargot
(1985)

Clovis Crawfish and His Friends
(1985)

Clovis Crawfish and the Curious Crapaud
(1986)

(Pelican Publishing Company is reissuing the earlier titles with new color and black-and-white illustrations as the original editions go out of print.)

Clovis Crawfish and the Curious Crapaud

Mary Alice Fontenot

Illustrated by Christine Kidder

PELICAN PUBLISHING COMPANY

GRETNA 1986

Library of Congress Cataloging-in-Publication Data

Fontenot, Mary Alice.
  Clovis Crawfish and the curious crapaud.

  Summary: Clovis must defend shy Corinne Crapaud
from the criticism of her cousin Fernand Frog.
  [1. Bayous—Fiction 2. Animals—Fiction]
I. Kidder, Christine, ill. II. Title.
PZ7.F73575Clk   1986   [Fic]   86-4997
ISBN 0-88289-610-5

Printed in Hong Kong by Everbest Printing Company, Ltd.
Through Four Color Imports, Ltd., Louisville, Kentucky
Published by Pelican Publishing Company, Inc.
1101 Monroe Street, Gretna, Louisiana 70053

For Deidre Foreman and Dan Hayes
Marraine *and* **Parrain**
of Corinne Crapaud

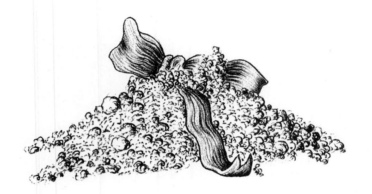

Clovis Crawfish liked rain. It made nice, soft mud. He crawled around on the muddy bayou bank and right over a big bump of mud.

The bump of mud shook and quivered. Clovis curled his tail under and backed up. His big, sharp claws opened wide.

The bump of mud hopped right over Clovis.

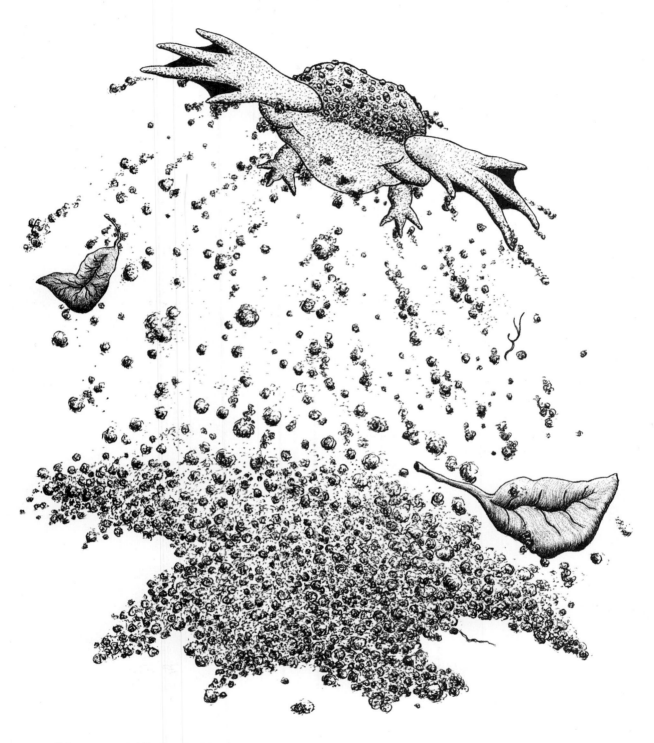

"*Guette-là!*" said Clovis, which is the way Louisiana Acadians say, "Watch it!" Clovis was so surprised his whiskers waved around fiercely and his big claws opened wider.

"*Mais jamais,* but it's not a bump of mud at all!" said Clovis. "It's a *crapaud,*" which is the way to say "toad-frog" in French.

Fernand, the big frog that lives in the bayou, hopped up on the bayou bank.

"That's my cousin, Corinne Crapaud," said Fernand. "She can't talk very well."

Corinne Crapaud began to puff up. She got bigger and bigger.

"I don't know why she does that," said Fernand. "Just look at her!"

"It's because you've hurt her feelings," Clovis told Fernand.
Corinne was so puffed up she was almost twice as big as she was before.

René Rainfrog hopped up, droplets of rain running off his bright green suit.

"*C'est vrai*, Clovis," said René, which means "It's true" in French. "She only knows five words, and they're all question words. How could I be kin to something so ugly and stupid!"

Corinne Crapaud puffed up some more.

Clovis snapped his claws at Fernand and René. *"Ta pas honte!"* he said, which means "Shame on you!" in Acadian-French. Fernand said *"Ouaouaron!"* in his big, deep voice and jumped back into the bayou. René Rainfrog hid himself on the underside of a fern frond.

Clovis crawled all around Corinne Crapaud, his tail making fan-shaped tracks in the soft mud.

"You really are the color of mud, Corinne," he said. "Me, I think mud is pretty."

Corinne began to unpuff herself a little.

Clovis folded his claws. "Don't be scared, Corinne," he said. "What you need is a friend."

"*Qui?*" said Corinne Crapaud, which means "Who?"

Fernand Frog poked his head out of the water. "You hear that, Clovis? That's one of her five words."

Corinne began to puff up again.

"Listen, Corinne, I have an idea," said Clovis.
"Quoi?" said Corinne, which is the French word for "What?"

René Rainfrog slithered around to the top side of the fern frond.
"Now she has only three words left!" he croaked.

Corinne Crapaud puffed up some more.

"Oh, my!" said Clovis. "We're going to have to do something to help you."

"*Pourquoi?*" said Corinne, which means "Why?"

Clovis wiggled his whiskers. "So your cousins won't talk about you and make you puff up. Do you think you could learn some new words?"

"Quand?" said Corinne, which means "When?"

Fernand Frog poked his head up. "That's four! That's four!" croaked Fernand.

"Only one more! Only one more!" chirped René Rainfrog.

Suddenly the rain came pouring down. Clovis's mud house began to melt. It got smaller and smaller until there was nothing left but a puddle of mud and the round hole in the ground.

Clovis looked at his melted mud house. "Now I'll have to build myself another house," he said.

"*Ou?*" said Corinne Crapaud, which means "Where?"

Fernand Frog popped up again. René Rainfrog hopped off the fern frond.

"*C'est tout!*" croaked Fernand, which means "That's all!"

"*C'est tout* for you, Corinne!" echoed René Rainfrog.

Corinne tried to hide herself in the hole in the middle of the puddle of mud, but she was so puffed up she got stuck.

"Prend courage, Corinne!" said Clovis, which is the way to say "Be brave" in French.

Chère Bebette

Piano arrangement
by Jeanne and Robert Gilmore

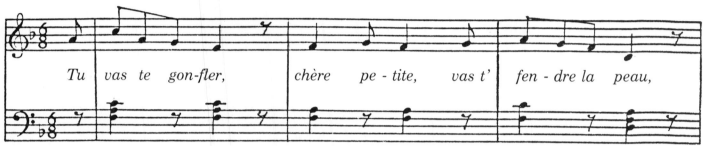

Tu vas te gon-fler, chère pe - tite, vas t' fen - dre la peau,

saute cra - paud. Je viens pour t'ai-der, Co- rinne, Co-rin-nette,

parce que je t'aime, chère be-bette.

Translation:

You're going to puff yourself up, dear little one,
You're going to split your skin, jump toadfrog.
I come to help you, Corinne, Corinnette,
Because I love you, dear little frog.

Poor Corinne! She wiggled and squirmed and squirmed and wiggled, but she couldn't get herself out of the hole. She was too puffed up.

Clovis Crawfish crawled up real close to where Corinne was stuck in the hole.

"You're not ugly and you're not stupid, Corinne," he said. "You need to learn some new words, that's all. I'll help you."

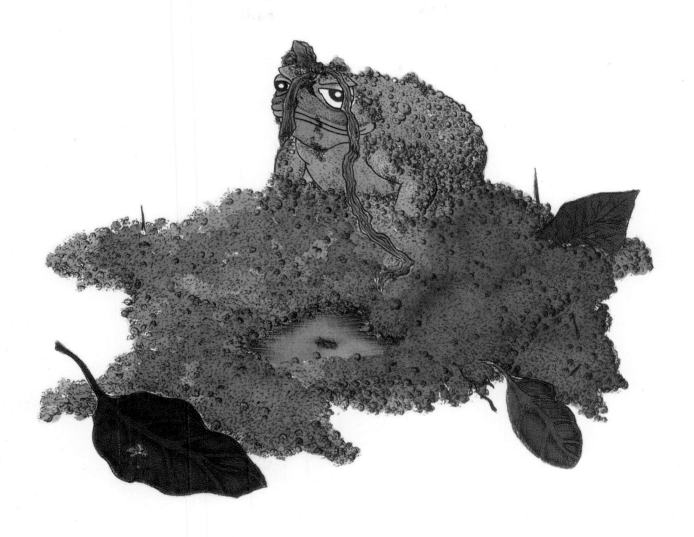

Corinne pushed and pulled and wriggled and squirmed, but she stayed stuck in the hole.

"*Chère* Corinne," said Clovis. "Please let me be your friend!"

Corinne stopped pushing and wiggling. She unpuffed herself all the way. Then it was easy for her to squirm out of the hole.

"I really like you, Corinne!" said Clovis.

Corinne blinked her big, round eyes. "*Combien?*" she said, which means "How much?"

Fernand Frog popped up. *"Bonjour,* little cousin!" he said.

René Rainfrog hopped back over the fern. "She learned a new word! She learned a new word!" he said. "Me, I come from a smart family!"

Corinne Crapaud hopped around happily. While she watched Clovis Crawfish build himself a new house, she practiced all of her six question words six times each.